PERSEVERE
&
PURSUE

Do What is in Your Heart to Do

Yolanda
Radford-Sartin

Persevere & Pursue – Do What is in Your Heart to Do

Scriptures marked KJV are taken from the KING JAMES VERSION (KJV): KING JAMES VERSION, public domain.

Scriptures marked NIV are taken from the NEW INTERNATIONAL VERSION Copyright© 1973, 1978, 1984, 2011 by Biblica, Inc.™. Used by permission of Zondervan.

Scriptures marked NKJV are taken from the NEW KING JAMES VERSION (NKJV): Scripture taken from the NEW KING JAMES VERSION®. Copyright© 1982 by Thomas Nelson, Inc. Used by permission.

Scriptures marked (NLT) are taken from the Holy Bible, New Living Translation, copyright © 1996, 2004, 2007, 2013, 2015 by Tyndale House Foundation. Used by permission of Tyndale House Publishers, Inc., Carol Stream, Illinois 60188.

Scriptures marked TM are taken from the THE MESSAGE: THE BIBLE IN CONTEMPORARY ENGLISH (TM): Scripture taken from THE MESSAGE: THE BIBLE IN CONTEMPORARY ENGLISH, copyright©1993, 1994, 1995, 1996, 2000, 2001, 2002. Used by permission of NavPress Publishing Group.

ISBN: 978-1-952327-94-0
Library of Congress Control Number: 2020903553
Printed in the United States of America

T.A.L.K. Publishing, LLC
talkconsulting.net

To Readers of Persevere and Pursue

A vision God has given me
Is to publish books of poetry

To inspire the soul and motivate the mind
And pierce the hearts of all humankind

The books I will publish in the name of Jesus Christ
Are of inspirational poetry God has inspired me to write

These books will be available in various book stores
Throughout the United States and across the ocean shores

Lost souls will be filled with the spirit of Christ
And a desire to live a righteous life

They will seek a desire to be set free
And cry out to the Lord God Almighty

When you read this book, take your time
May the spirit, through which it was written
Will pierce your heart and mind

Sincerely, The Author
Yolanda Radford-Sartin

"Commit thy way unto the Lord; trust also in him;
and he shall bring it to pass."
Psalm 37:5, King James Version (KJV)

Dedication

I
dedicate
this book to
my loving and supportive
mother, Malvenie,
and the memory of my loving
father, Curtis.

Acknowledgments

I give all the glory and honor to God for providing me
the endurance to persevere
significant life challenges
and pursue what He put in my heart to do.

****

I give special thanks to the Author Lab for
facilitating the process to
Write, Print, and Publish in 90 Days.
God's timing is perfect.

****

I give special thanks to my loving husband
Deon M. Sartin for his patience,
support, and consistent encouragement.

****

I would also like to give special thanks
to my Pastor, Melva Henderson,
for her assistance, words of wisdom, and prayers.

Poetry to Persevere and Pursue

Introduction

In the process of pursuing what was in my heart, I found myself
faced with unexpected challenges along the way, like being
diagnosed with breast cancer just five short months after my mother
(mom). Placing my father in a nursing home due to complications
with the advanced stages of Alzheimer's Disease, a career change,
and returning to college to earn my master's degree in Nursing
Education.

To persevere, I had to look beyond the circumstances drawing divine
strength and wisdom to conquer the challenges. At the onset, I chose
to depend on the word of God, scriptures like Philippians 4:13 NLT,
which states, *"I can do all things through Christ who gives me
strength."* and others like it. I have chosen to share my story,
utilizing poetry, the word of God, and reflection questions. I believe
the contents of this book will uplift your spirit, inspire your heart,
motivate your mind, and impact your life. The anointing of God
saturates every page. As you read, expect to experience God's peace,
love, power, strength, wisdom, revelation, and joy. It is my prayer
that you will choose to pursue your highest goals and dreams despite
life's challenges, believing *"with God, nothing is impossible."* (Luke
1:37)

As you read this book, I pray you will see yourself walking in peace,
overcoming obstacles, and demonstrating a higher level of self-
confidence. I want to encourage you to take the time to answer the
reflection questions as they will help you see what is in your heart.
As you read this book, I declare the Spirit of God will help you
Persevere and Pursue what is in your heart with peace.

Your Dream

Live life to the fullest
From day to day
Conquer every challenge
That comes your way

Visualize your dream
Hold it in your mind
Attaining your dream
Is just a matter of time

Tell yourself
You will succeed
Negative affirmations
You do not need

People will get jealous
And envious of you
Press on with pride
There is nothing you can't do

If you stumble
And fall to the ground
Jump to your feet
Continuing forward bound

The dream you have
Make it come true
You have what it takes
Just Believe in you

No matter how rocky
The road may seem
Work each day towards
Attaining your dream

What is your dream? What do you want to do? Where do you want to go? Is there a city, country, or region of the world that you've always wanted to travel, but for some reason, have never taken the time to plan? Is there something in your heart at this point in your life that you've always wanted to do but haven't pursued? Things like starting your own business, taking a class to learn a foreign language, pursuing your desire to sing, becoming a life coach, returning to school, teaching others how to play an instrument, or writing a book. Whatever your passion, I encourage you to pursue it without regard for your age, or those who may have discouraged you saying you couldn't do it. Persevere, pursue, make a choice to never give up on you.

Regardless of what may have happened in your life up to this point, or how challenging obstacles may have been to overcome, you have the power to step beyond the chains and restrictions of the past.

Permit yourself to take a moment to look deep inside your heart, asking yourself a question, *"What is my dream?"* Write your answer on the reflection page.

Reflection Questions

What is your Dream? Think about it. Write it down.

_____

_____

_____

_____

_____

_____

_____

_____

_____

_____

_____

Describe what it would feel like to live your dream. Think about it. Write it down.

_____

_____

_____

_____

_____

_____

_____

_____

_____

_____

Prayer of Thanks

God, I thank you for Your love
I thank you for the power of prayer
When I cry out to You Heavenly Father
I can depend on You to be there

You hear me when I cry
With compassion, you acknowledge my plea
I praise You for Your mercy and grace
My Father God Almighty

You wipe away the tears
And fill my heart with joy
It is Your will to have Your way
In every man woman girl and boy

I thank you for Your Spirit
That guides me along the way
I thank you for Your Word
That orders my steps from day to day

I thank you for Your peace
To persevere and pursue
I thank you for the wisdom
To do what is in my heart to do

I thank you for the challenges
I will face along the way
I give you the glory for the victory
In Jesus' name, I pray.
Amen

My parents taught my siblings and me about God and His precious Son, Jesus Christ. They instilled in us the importance of prayer. I remember as a child before going to bed, my sister, being the eldest, would lead my brothers and me in prayer on our knees at the side of the bed. At family gatherings, my father or uncle led the family in prayer. As you can see, prayer has always been a fundamental part of my heritage.

As I look back on my life: placing my father in a nursing home, being diagnosed with breast cancer five months after my mother's breast cancer diagnosis, I can do nothing except give God the glory for walking with me, every step of the way. It was not easy, but it was my journey, one I chose to walk through, leaning on God and His word.

Reflection Questions

What challenges are you currently facing? Think about it. Write it down.

_____

_____

_____

_____

_____

_____

_____

_____

_____

_____

What will you do to overcome those challenges? Think about it. Write it down.

_____

_____

_____

_____

_____

_____

_____

_____

_____

_____

You Have My Word

(A message from the Spirit of God)

As you read My word from day to day
I will speak to your spirit in a supernatural way

Take heed to what your spirit will receive
What I reveal to you others will need

Do not be surprised at what I have for you to do
My spirit will lead and guide you into all truth

There is healing in your hands and power in your tongue
Move out of my way there is work to be done

People are dying open your eyes and see
They need My word to be delivered and set free

You have holy ghost boldness and power from above
To speak My word with compassion and love

I will use you for My glory My word is alive
Without My Word, you cannot survive

Stand firm in My word and the power of My might
I will be with you morning, noon and night

No weapon formed against you shall prosper or succeed
You have my word, and that is all you need

The word of God is my number one source of wisdom, provision, strength, and peace. During the most challenging times in my life, when I needed help beyond my ability, I found it in the word of God.

The Word never fails. It is reliable, dependable, trustworthy and true. For me, God's word is an absolute necessity.

To secure victory:

- **You will need God's wisdom t**o know what to do. According to James 1:5 NLT, *"If you need wisdom, ask our generous God and he will give it to you. He will not rebuke you for asking."*

- **You will need God's promise of provision** to ensure every need is met along the way. Meditate on Philippians 4:19 NLT. *"And this same God who takes care of me will supply all your needs from his glorious riches, which have been given to us in Christ Jesus."*

- **You will need God's strength** in moments of weakness. The circumstances of life can be physically and emotionally draining, and you may feel the urge to quit. In those moments, find strength in scriptures such as Psalms 18:32 NLT, *"God arms me with strength, and he makes my way perfect";* and Psalms 46:1 NLT *"God is our refuge and strength, always ready to help in times of trouble."*

- **You will need God's peace t**o fill your heart and mind when the report is unfavorable. Philippians 4:7 NLT *"Then you will experience God's peace, which exceeds anything we can understand. His peace will guard your hearts and minds as you live in Christ Jesus."* When your mind is on everything going on around you, and your thoughts are consumed by the needs of others, anxiety, and confusion can enter into the heart. To maintain inner peace and cope effectively, keep your mind on the word of God.

- **You will need God's healing power** to be a reality in your body and those you love: *I will give you back your health and heal your wounds, says the Lord."* Jeremiah 30:17 NLT *"The Lord nurses them when they are sick and restores them to health."* Psalm 41:3 NLT. God is the Great Physician. He is the healer who gives doctors the wisdom to practice medicine. Knowing this when faced with my fight of faith, I took the time to pray with and for every nurse and doctor who had a hand in providing care for my family and me.

Reflection Questions

What do you lean on, or who do you look to in times of trouble?
Think about it. Write it down.

_____

_____

_____

_____

_____

_____

_____

_____

_____

_____

_____

_____

_____

_____

_____

_____

_____

_____

_____

_____

_____

My Father

My father was a Blessing
Sent from God above
He honored my mom as his wife
His family he truly loved

He taught me self-respect
And the difference between right and wrong
When times were hard and I wanted to give up
He was there to say hold on

He was a tremendous influence
In my life in many ways
He is one of the reasons
I am who I am today

Fathers are important people
Through the eyes of a precious child
The quality time they spend with them
Is time spent worthwhile

I am thankful for the time I had with my dad
I can close my eyes and see
I had a father who loved the Lord
And wanted God's best for me

My father was a clean-cut, handsome man who loved his family. He was an eloquent speaker who was called upon often to write and deliver speeches at various church functions. From a very early age, my father recognized that I shared the gift of writing and encouraged me to write. He was also a poet who could articulate beautiful poetry without writing it on paper.

My father was very attentive to my mother. When my father would hear her arriving home after dark, he would open the door and assist her in the house. When my mother cooked large meals, my father would sit at the kitchen table to keep her company no matter how long she took. He didn't cook much, but he was willing to wash dishes.

My father was a hard-working man. He maintained his job until my mother encouraged him to retire after working for nearly thirty-four years. Within a couple of years of his retirement, my mother noticed my father becoming forgetful. He would misplace his keys. My mother or brother would find them in the door or the ignition of the car. He would put away household items and blame my brothers or me for moving them when he could not find them. Considering my father's increased episodes of forgetfulness, she wanted him to be able to retire with dignity versus getting fired due to carelessness. As time went on we learned that my father had Alzheimer's disease.

One afternoon my eldest brother paid a visit to my parents' home. While there, he and my mother assisted my father, who battled memory loss due to the progression of Alzheimer's disease. My father needed assistance every step of the way, from undressing himself, to stepping into the bathtub. On this particular day, my brother made sure my father was secure in the shower and headed home. After forty-five minutes, my mother called him, saying, *"Your dad will not get out of the shower!"* I lived five minutes away, so my brother contacted me, and I immediately headed to my parent's home. I remember my heart racing while driving. My prayer was, *"Lord, give me Your wisdom. Help us with my dad."* When I arrived, I rushed to the bathroom only to discover my father lost his ability to follow simple instructions. He just stood, staring, looking straight ahead as though paralyzed. My mother looked at me with deep concern in her eyes and with a worried voice saying, *"Your dad will not move. He won't let me help him get out of the shower."*

I knew what I needed to do, but for some reason, I needed proof. My first response was to call Melba, a friend, and fellow nurse whose mother also struggled with memory loss. Melba gave me the confirmation I needed. I took a deep breath and dialed 911. While the phone was ringing, I thought to myself, *"God won't put more on us than we can handle."* In the meantime, my mother remained with my father in the bathroom. Within minutes, I could hear the sirens of the fire truck and ambulance blaring through the neighborhood. When the emergency responders arrived, I directed them to the bathroom where my father was. After assessing the situation, they decided to place a chair in the bathtub and guided my father to a seated position. They proceeded to cover him with a blanket. It took three emergency responders to safely lift my father out of the bathtub, from the chair to the ambulance stretcher as they took my father from our family home. I held tightly to my mother before we headed for the hospital.

Reflective Questions

Would you have the capacity to give of yourself if they needed you? Think about it. Write it down.

_____

_____

_____

_____

_____

_____

_____

_____

_____

_____

_____

_____

_____

_____

_____

_____

_____

_____

_____

_____

_____

_____

When Trying Times Arise

Cast your cares upon the Lord
For you, He truly cares
God does not expect you to handle
More than you can bear

God created you in His likeness
He sent His son in the image of a man
Because of Christ when trials arise
You have the strength to stand

The joy of the Lord is your strength
He alone is all you need
When trying times arise
Choose to praise God Almighty

Keep your focus on the Lord
And what He can do
During the most challenging and trying times
His Spirit will comfort you

No matter how difficult the situation maybe
With God, the victory is won
With God in control of your circumstances
His divine will be done

My father's complications with Alzheimer's disease came while I attended school full time in pursuit of my Master's Degree in nursing education and while working full-time as a nursing instructor at the Milwaukee Area Technical College. I went to the hospital daily to spend time with my father and assist the nursing staff with his care. The most challenging part of dealing with my father's condition was keeping him clean and dry. Incontinence is a common problem for those in the advanced stages of Alzheimer's Disease.

There were times when my father resisted the nursing staff; however, when I arrived, he became more compliant. There were also instances when even I walked away, frustrated, and in tears asking for God's help. Through His grace, I was strengthened and given the ability to approach my father with a more considerable measure of compassion and patience.

My father did not realize where he was, but he knew his current location was not his home, and unfortunately, he would never go back to his house. While in the care of the hospital, I had the daunting task of finding a nursing home that provided high-quality care to its residents. My mother and siblings wanted a facility near my parents' house. Unfortunately, I visited several nursing homes and left many in tears due to the conditions and poor quality of care. It was heartbreaking for my family to go through this process, but we could no longer provide safe care at home. Before that day, my father would leave out of the house and wander away from home. For his safety, the locks on all the doors were changed.

It was hard to leave my father day after day while he was in the hospital. My mother and I usually left after he went to sleep, and I would follow my mother's home, ensuring her safety. I generally walked through my doors between 9:00 and 10:00 pm. Once home, I would do a final nightly check-in with my mother, take a brief moment to unwind, grab a bite to eat, complete homework, then get up the next morning only to start over again. At the start of each day, I spent time in the Word of God. I read scriptures on strength. Those like those found in 2 Corinthians 2:9 NLT *"His strength is made perfect in weakness."* I needed the power of God to go through and endure each day. When I began to think about my dad's situation and how hard it was on my mom, my heart became heavy, and my eyes welled with tears. I had to take control of my thoughts by taking a moment to meditate on the word of God. It gave me peace and renewed my mind. I would then begin to thank God for taking me through. No matter what you encounter, be encouraged to walk with the word of God, believing you can do all things through Christ, who strengthens you.

Reflective Questions

How would you handle an unexpected disruption in your life? Think about it. Write it down.

_____

_____

_____

_____

_____

_____

_____

_____

_____

_____

_____

_____

_____

_____

_____

_____

_____

_____

_____

_____

_____

Walking with God

Trust in the Lord will all your heart
Cast upon Him your care
During challenging times, you are not alone
The spirit of peace is there

Trust in the Lord with all your heart
Choose not to walk in fear
Allow the word of God to renew your mind
And His love to dry your tears

When you don't have the answers
The word of God will speak to you
His presence during the circumstances
Will strengthen and carry you through

Trust in the Lord with all your heart
He is the provider of your every need
Praise God in spirit and truth
Your praise confuses the enemy

When you are walking with God, you are more equipped
To handle what comes your way
When you walk with God trust, believe
And have faith when you pray

To walk with God is a choice. When you make a choice, it requires absolute trust. Trust in God's word, trust in God's promises, trust in God's ability to do what He said He would do. I chose to trust and believe God's word, and in doing so, His faithfulness stood firm in the most significant challenges of my life. God carried us through.

I recall, one evening, while my father was in the hospital, standing over my mother, who was seated in a kitchen chair. As we sorted through my parent's mail, I looked down to ask a question and noticed a drop of blood on her T-Shirt at her left nipple site. I asked, *"Mom, what is that?"* She replied, *"I don't know. I am not eating or drinking anything."* I then said, *"Mom, that looks like blood. We need to get that checked out."* Prior too, my mother hadn't noticed any drainage from her breast nor any after that evening. The next day I was able to get an early appointment within three days of the call. My parents were rarely apart from each other for any significant amount of time. They did everything together. My mom felt as though she needed to be at the hospital each morning when he woke. Although not surprised, the night before the appointment, my mom suggested that I reschedule. She was determined to be at the hospital first thing in the morning. Reluctantly I canceled the appointment and scheduled it for the following week. My mom's focus was on my dad and working with the hospital social worker to find the right nursing home. We chose to believe God would work everything out on behalf of my mother.

Reflection Questions

Describe a time in your life when you struggled to trust God. Think about it. Write it down.

_____

_____

_____

_____

_____

_____

_____

_____

_____

_____

_____

_____

_____

_____

_____

_____

_____

_____

_____

_____

_____

As You Wait

Waiting can be hard to do
Patience is the key
Stay focused on the process
Of waiting on God Almighty

He always shows up
God is never late
It may seem like forever
When you choose to wait

Wait on the information
Wait to know what to do
Wait to receive clear directions
To wait may be challenging for you

Be anxious for nothing says the Lord
Submit all to Him in prayer
He knows what you are going through
As you go, He is there

As you wait, take time to pray
As you wait, seek His face
As you wait, study His Word
And hear what God has to say

God is always speaking
Be encouraged to anticipate
Receiving everything you need from God
When you take the time to wait

A week after I noticed the drop of blood on my mother's shirt, I accompanied my mother to her doctor's appointment. During the visit, the doctor saw the left nipple appearing to be slightly irregular. She prescribed a topical cream for two weeks. After week one, there were no apparent changes in the appearance of my mother's breast. Concerned, I made a follow-up call to her doctor informing her of my observations. The doctor immediately scheduled a mammogram and ultrasound for the next day. Ironically, before this discovery, for nearly two years, my mother received a mammogram every six months. However, her doctor never expressed concern regarding the results.

Seven days after the mammogram and ultrasound, my mother's results came in. When we arrived at the hospital, instead of meeting the doctor who ordered the tests, we were informed that the appointment would be with a surgeon. I thought to myself, *"Why are we meeting with a surgeon?"* I was not at peace about this. The surgeon walked into the room with my mother's chart, sat in a chair, and began to speak to my mother as though she was the only person in the room. I interjected in a matter of fact way, *"Hello, I am Yolanda, Malvenie's daughter!"*

He looked at me and said, *"Hello,"* and continued paging through my mom's chart. He then proceeded to state, *"I removed a cyst from your right breast five years ago."* He continued to make several comments about her medical history.

Annoyed, I listened to his questions, thinking to myself, *"My mom is seventy-two years old."* I then stated with a stern voice, *"My mother's health history has not changed. We are here to discuss the results of the mammogram and ultrasound."* The doctor remained silent, and I became utterly irritated. The surgeon finally spoke up, saying the test results were inconclusive. However, he wanted to schedule a biopsy of her left nipple *"in about two weeks."* I said to myself, *"Two weeks is too long to wait to schedule a biopsy."* As soon as we left his office, I looked at mom and said, *"We are not coming back here."*

My mom replied, *"Okay, now let's go see your daddy."*

Reflection Questions

What do you do when a circumstance requires you to wait patiently? Think about it. Write it down.

_____

_____

_____

_____

_____

_____

_____

_____

_____

_____

_____

_____

_____

_____

_____

_____

_____

_____

_____

_____

_____

_____

_____

God Can Do Anything but Fail

Let the spirit of God speak to your heart
Let His will for your life prevail
Let the Word of God manifest through you
God can do anything but fail

Trust and depend on what God says
In your life let Him have His way
Meditate on the Word as you walk with the Lord
In the spirit day after day

Focus on the Word of God
When you go through trying times
The power in the Word of God
Brings peace to your heart and mind

Satan will flood your mind with fear and doubt
He wants complete control
But the weapons of our warfare are mighty through God
To the pulling down of strongholds

Apply the Word of God to your circumstances
His Word by faith will prevail
The awesome, mighty God we serve
Can do anything but fail

My mother and I left her doctor's appointment and went directly to visit my father. Upon our arrival at the hospital, I ran into my father's social worker. In a brief conversation, she confirmed my father's discharge plans to a nursing facility near my mother's house. My heart immediately filled with joy. I took a deep breath, exhaled, and began to thank God. He is a way-maker. Only God can make a way out where there seems to be no way. The God who never fails.

After my conversation with the social worker, my mind shifted to my mother. I began to think about the surgeon's comments and his projected plan for her. As I continued to walk down the hall, I asked the Lord, *"What should I do? Who should I call?"* I wanted a second opinion but did not know where to begin. No sooner than I asked those questions, the Spirit of God, who leads and guides me into all truth, led me to call a dear friend, Phyllis Holder. Phyllis was a retired nursing instructor as well as a breast cancer survivor. When I spoke with her, she was more than willing to provide her assistance. She recommended an excellent doctor, who happened to be the Director of the Breast Care Center at the same hospital caring for my father. After speaking with Phyllis, I immediately called, and to my surprise, my mother was scheduled for an appointment that same week. I am happy to say that when we arrived at the Breast Care Center, the doctor who saw my mom had excellent bedside manners. She briefly examined my mom and ordered an MRI of her left breast.

Reflection Questions

What do you need to pursue with persistence? Think about it. Write it down.

_____

_____

_____

_____

_____

_____

_____

_____

What three things will you do to demonstrate your persistence? Think about it. Write it down.

_____

_____

_____

_____

_____

_____

_____

_____

_____

_____

When God Speaks

God is speaking all the time
He is in your spirit and on your mind

He is with you wherever you go
When you study His Word, spiritually, you grow

God fills your heart with joy and peace
When you cry out to Him, He hears your plea

Speak His promises expecting to be heard
God looks for opportunities to perform His Word

When God speaks to your heart, He stirs your soul
He enables you to stand firm, tall and bold

I have learned to apply God's Word to my life,
And praise Him for the victory in the name of Jesus Christ

I have learned what it means to walk by faith
And give glory to God for His amazing grace

He is your refuge, your strength, and strong tower
With God, you have wisdom, knowledge, peace, and power

My heart is in tune, and my spirit is at peace
When I listen to God and take heed when He speaks

When God speaks to your heart, listen and receive
Direction from the Father with humility

One evening while at work with a clinical group of nursing students, I felt my phone vibrating in my pocket. I was anticipating a call from the doctor with the results of my mother's MRI. I walked to an empty room to answer the phone. It was the hospital calling. Anxious to hear what the doctor would say, I took a deep breath and answered. In a serious yet calm tone of voice, the doctor stated that the MRI did reveal cancer cells in my mom's left breast. I took another deep breath, exhaled, and asked the doctor to repeat what she said. I was on the phone for several minutes, asking questions and receiving information regarding the next steps for my mom. I ended the call while trying to maintain my composure, and dialed my pastor, Melva Henderson. After sharing the report of the doctor, she responded by acknowledging the MRI results but with a sternness equal to that of the doctor, proceeded to remind me that God was greater than cancer. She shared healing scriptures and prayed for my mom. My pastor's words resonated deep within me. I knew God had spoken. So before returning to the students, I took a moment to focus my mind on verses of scripture I meditated before that day.

"And the peace of God, which surpasses all understanding, will guard your hearts and minds through Christ Jesus."
Philippians 4:7 NLT.

"Trust in the Lord with all your heart; do not depend on your understanding. Seek his will in all you do, and he will show you which path to take."
Proverbs 3:5-6 NLT.

Reflection Questions

Is there a time you can remember hearing the voice of God through another person? What did He say? Think about it. Write it down.

_____

_____

_____

_____

_____

_____

_____

_____

_____

_____

_____

_____

_____

_____

_____

_____

_____

_____

_____

_____

_____

The Voice of God

Listen for the voice of God
Listen when He speaks
Be still and know the voice of God
It is the voice of clarity

God's voice is the voice of wisdom
God's voice is light when it's dark
God's voice gave Noah specific direction
On when where and how to build the ark

The voice of God spoke the beginning
The voice of God spoke the end
The voice of God speaks to you
As a father and a friend

In the voice of God, there is peace
In the voice of God, there is power
The voice of God can transform your life
No matter the day time or the hour

Position yourself to hear from God
Position yourself to be still
Position yourself to receive from God
Position yourself to be filled

Filled with the anointed power of God
Filled with His love
Filled with His wisdom, compassion, and grace
To be a blessing from God above

It was the Word of God that carried me to the end of my workday and the peace of God that accompanied me on my journey to my mother's home. Upon arrival, my mother was sitting on the couch watching television. As she stood to greet me, mom noticed my somber disposition. With a warm, embracing hug, she asked, *"What's wrong?"* I grabbed her hand, gently pulled her toward the couch, and proceeded to share the report of the doctor. I will never forget my mother's response; all she said was, *"Okay."* Taken back by her simple reaction, all I could think to say was, *"What!?"* I immediately noted that my mother was not moved by what she heard. I soon discovered my mom had inside information.

Earlier that day, as mom was leaving the nursing home visiting my father, she said a voice told her, *"I am your only source."* When she heard these words, mom said she stopped in her tracks. Mom continued sharing, *"When I looked to the left and then to the right and saw that no one else was there, I quickly realized that God was speaking to me."* She said she regained her focus and continued out the door walking in the strength of God. My mother believed everything was going to be alright. She could have chosen to ignore the voice of God leaving the nursing home with her head down, considering everything going on in her life at that time. Instead, my mother decided to yield to the spoken Word of God, trusting His voice, believing His promises.

"The voice of the Lord is powerful; the voice of the Lord is majestic."
Psalm 29:4 NLT.

Reflection Questions

How do you respond to the voice of God? Think about it. Write it down.

_____

_____

_____

_____

_____

_____

_____

_____

_____

_____

_____

_____

_____

_____

_____

_____

_____

_____

_____

_____

_____

Focus on the Word

When you go through trying times
Look past what you see
Don't focus on your circumstances
Focus on God Almighty

When you go through trying times
Don't focus on what others may say
Focus on the Word of God
And the message He conveys

When you go through trying times
Don't focus on how you feel
Put your trust and faith in the Word of God
For by His stripes you are healed

Saturate your mind with the Word of God
Morning, noon and night
Do not be distracted by your circumstances
Walk by faith and not by sight

Your load may be heavy
When it seems too much to bear
Turn to your heavenly father who said
Cast upon Me your care

He said I will carry the load for you
When you are weak say, I'm strong
Only God can make everything right
When everything appears to be going wrong

Put your trust and faith in God Almighty
Open your heart and mind to receive
For all things are possible
Unto Him who believes

It was the power in the Word of God that carried us through my mother's breast cancer diagnosis and my father's transition from home, to hospital, to a nursing facility. Within two weeks of my mother's diagnosis, she underwent a lumpectomy, a surgical procedure to remove cancerous tissue from the breast. Thank God, as expected, there were no post-surgical complications. The day after surgery, the surgeon visited my mother and was surprised at her progress. She could raise her left arm over her head without pain; mom was ready to get back to her life. My mom informed the doctor of her need to leave the hospital to check on her husband. She told the doctor, *"Everything is going to be alright."* Mom had a persevering mindset. The day she was discharged from the hospital, I took her to the nursing home to see my dad at her request.

Looking back, God's grace to go through was amazing. Grace enabled me to walk with my parents and complete critical assignments for my master's degree. There were times when I did not know how they were going to get done. However, in the midst of it all, I pursued with persistence.

Reflection Questions

Are you familiar with the Grace of God in your life? Can you share a time when an outcome should have been different, but because of Grace, it worked in your favor? Think about it. Write it down.

_____

_____

_____

_____

_____

_____

_____

_____

_____

_____

_____

_____

_____

_____

_____

_____

_____

_____

_____

_____

_____

Look Beyond the Circumstances

When situations arise
Beyond your repair
Look beyond the circumstances
And know God is there

Look beyond what you see
Bypass the fear and doubt
Praise God in the situation
And expect Him to work it out

Put your trust and faith in the father
What do the scriptures say
Apply the Word of God
To your circumstances each day

Whatever you are going through
It doesn't matter what it may be
When you let go and give it to God
He will provide you with His peace

Look beyond your ability
Look at what God can do
Look beyond the circumstances
And see God strengthening you

With God nothing is impossible
Through Him, all things can be done
When you walk with God, believe by faith
The victory is won

My mother received a stage two breast cancer diagnosis at the age of seventy-two. She received about four rounds of chemotherapy and radiation treatments every morning for six weeks, and God allowed me to attend every appointment with her. I prayed for my mom and the doctors, physically holding hands before every procedure. I viewed the doctors as God's conduit of healing for my mother. As a result, the God who never fails worked on my mother's behalf. Although she lost all of her hair, my mother did not experience any other adverse side effects of chemotherapy or radiation treatments. She looked beyond her circumstances, keeping her eyes fixed on the promise God made to her. To date, mom is a vibrant woman with a beautiful head of long hair. To God, be the glory!

Reflection Questions

What circumstances do you need to look beyond?
Think about it. Write it down.

_____

_____

_____

_____

_____

_____

_____

_____

_____

How will you prepare yourself to conquer difficult situations when they arise? Think about it. Write it down.

_____

_____

_____

_____

_____

_____

_____

_____

_____

_____

_____

This Too Shall Pass

During your situation
In the middle of all you do
When the load appears to heavy to bear
God's strength will carry you

He knows what you are going through
He has you where you are
He has chosen you; you will endure
Depend on Him by far

Be encouraged in your circumstances
Especially when things go wrong
Your faith in God, your trust in Him
Is what will keep you strong

You may feel you are all alone
Just believe God is there
You are encouraged by the Holy Spirit
To cast upon Him your cares

I pray you are filled with joy and peace
In Jesus name that will always last
This may be a challenging time for you
But know this too shall pass

When we decide to walk by faith, it's essential to understand that no circumstance will last forever. When we're faced with situations that seem unbearable or they linger on, we must remember that God is faithful, true to His Word. He's made what the bible calls exceeding great and precious promises, such as, *"No temptation has overtaken you except what is common to mankind. And God is faithful; he will not let you be tempted beyond what you can bear. But when you are tempted, he will also provide a way out so that you can endure it."*

(1 Corinthians 10:13 NIV) God has promised not to allow any circumstance to hit your life that you won't have the grace (ability) to endure or overcome. In other words, your problems will never outdo God's grace!

In February of 2008, five months after my mother's diagnosis of breast cancer, I had a follow-up appointment with my OBGYN to resolve issues with decreased iron levels and extreme fatigue resulting from fibroid tumors. In preparation for this appointment, the Spirit of the Lord led me to write a list of questions to ask the doctor. Oddly, one had nothing to do with my gynecological health. Upon meeting with the doctor, I felt a great urgency to ask for a mammogram. Understandably, considering my mother's recent diagnosis. Although breast health was not my doctor's specialty, she answered all of my questions, took heed to my concerns, and ordered a mammogram.

Four days later, at the age of thirty-nine, I had my first mammogram. The exam went well. The radiology technician relayed the message from the radiologist, saying, *"We will see you back in one year."*

I was relieved to hear those words. However, when I arrived home that afternoon, I had this message on my answering machine: *"Yolanda, this is a doctor from St Luke's radiology department. One of the doctors told you that everything was fine; however, the radiologist took a second read of the mammogram and noticed some calcifications that needed magnification, so we need to schedule a repeat mammogram."*

When I received that message, I immediately called the radiology department. However, the office closed for the day. I paged the on-call radiologist but didn't receive a callback until the next morning. When the radiologist did finally reach back, I missed his call. I then returned his call feeling like we were playing a game of phone tag. I was in no mood for playing games. I connected with the radiology department the following Monday to reschedule. I underwent my second mammogram a week later. The results were inconclusive, which meant I needed a biopsy. Deep in my heart, I believed, this too shall pass.

My prayer was, *"Lord, please lead and guide moving forward, in the name of Jesus, Amen."*

Reflections Questions

Have you ever had an experience when fear tried to overtake your mind? Think about it. Write it down.

_____

_____

_____

_____

_____

_____

_____

_____

_____

_____

_____

_____

_____

_____

_____

_____

_____

_____

_____

_____

_____

_____

_____

Too Heavy for Me

There is so much going on inside of me
Lord, I desire to be in perfect peace

Please show me how to handle what is going on
Strengthen me Lord and help me to be strong

I want to acknowledge all that is there
And cast upon You all of my care

Allow me to release what I feel inside
From You Dear God I cannot hide

My load appears to be too heavy for me
But nothing is too heavy or you God Almighty

I thank You right now for bringing me out
Giving me peace and removing the doubt

I praise You O'Lord in the midst of it all
Knowing if I stumble you will not let me fall

I am more than a conqueror I am heir to Your throne
I thank You the Holy Spirit with you I am never alone

On March 6, 2008, I had a core biopsy, which is a procedure where a needle is passed through the skin of the breast to take a sample of tissue. The tissue is then examined under a microscope for any abnormalities. During this time, I thought about planning my fortieth birthday gathering but quickly changed my mind considering all the medical testing I had to endure. When I shared this thought with my cousin LaShawn, she said, *"Yo, I will do it, send me the names."* I will never forget her words, *"I will do it."*

On March 7, 2008, while in the beauty shop, I just finished getting my hair done, when I received a phone call from the hospital. I will never forget that phone call. Why? Because I received it one week before my 40th Birthday. Yes, the doctor told me I had breast cancer. As I stood there, my reply was, *"What did you say?"*

She went on to say, *"The biopsy showed a very early stage of breast cancer."* Bewildered, I asked again, *"What did you say?"*

She said, *"If you are going to have breast cancer, this is the best kind to have - Ductal Cell Carcinoma Insitu."*

All I heard was *"BREAST CANCER."* I then said, *"Can you please repeat everything you just said so I could write it down?"*

Before ending the conversation, she told me that an appointment was scheduled for me to see a breast cancer surgeon, Dr. Judy Tjoe, at Aurora Sinai Medical Center the following Tuesday.

While trying to maintain my composure, I began to feel a heaviness inside. I ended the call by saying, *"Thank you."* I quickly paid the beautician and rushed to my car. As I left the parking lot, tears began to roll down my face. As thoughts of my mom and dad crossed my mind, I called one of my prayer partners, Charlotte Green. When she answered the phone, I shared with her what the doctor said in an extremely emotional way. I began to cry. I thought, *"If I had to have surgery, who would do what I do for my mom and dad."*

Charlotte lovingly reminded me, *"God is the healer of every sickness and disease. The doctors have their reports, but we are going to believe the report of the Lord."* She shared more scriptures with me, then she prayed. I believed she could sense the heaviness I was feeling in my heart. However, after she prayed, I experienced God's peace.

Reflective Questions

What would you do if you received a devastating report?
Think about it. Write it down.

_____

_____

_____

_____

_____

_____

_____

_____

_____

_____

_____

_____

_____

_____

_____

_____

_____

_____

_____

_____

_____

_____

When You Pray

The Bible says, Pray without ceasing
Talk to the Father in prayer
It is not God's will for you to worry
He said to cast upon Him your care

Call on God, and He will answer
And show you things you didn't know where there
When you pray, believe you receive
Trust God. There is power in prayer

When you pray, ask in Faith
When you ask, do not doubt
When you pray God will give you peace
And strength to walk it out

When you don't know what to say
Or exactly what to do
There is nothing wrong with asking someone
To fervently pray for you

The effectual fervent prayer of the righteous man
Avails much, this I believe
When you pray and do not doubt in your heart
What you pray expect to receive

Plan to expand your prayer life
There is power when you pray
When you are going through a challenging time
Choose to pray throughout your day

There is power in prayer. The Lord will give you His peace during a storm, and my storm was raging. My father was in a nursing home, and my mother was going through chemotherapy, and I, like my mother, had a diagnosis of breast cancer.

After the conversation with Charlotte, I proceeded to the nursing home. When I arrived, my dad was sitting in a chair. My mom was sitting on a chair next to him. I greeted them both with a hug and a kiss. I then sat on my father's bed. When my mom looked at me, she said: *"Yolanda, what's the matter?"* Hesitating, I looked at my mom and quietly told her that *"I received a call from the doctor while at the hair salon, and she said that I had breast cancer."* As my head dropped, my mom got out of her chair, hugged me, and said, *"My baby, my baby, it's going to be alright. We will get through this."*

I thank God for my mom. She was such a pillar of strength. We have learned to walk by faith and not by sight together. When I shared this with my mom, I made sure my dad did not hear what I said. Even though he had Alzheimer's, his thinking was apparent at times, and I didn't want him to worry about me. My mom and I agreed that we would not tell him. Dad went home to be with the Lord five months later, and we never did.

Reflection Questions

What is your prayer life like today? Think about it. Write it down.

_____

_____

_____

_____

_____

_____

_____

_____

_____

_____

_____

_____

_____

_____

_____

_____

_____

_____

_____

_____

_____

_____

_____

Make the Right Decision

To make the right decision
Is a difficult thing to do
Evaluate all your options
And choose what is best for you

To make the right decision
May take a very long time
Choose what you feel is right
Instead of relying on your mind

Thoughts come and go
They rarely remain the same
When feelings are strong in your heart
Strong feelings tend not to change

If you think you made the right decision
But feel it may be wrong
Turn to the Lord for guidance
And strength to carry-on

He will take away your worries
Pick you up when you're down
He will let you off your knees
And plant your feet on solid ground

He will take me by the hand
And walk with you in peace
He will shed light on your situation
Revealing how things should be

The Lord Almighty is perfect
There is nothing he can't do
He will help you make the right decision
The Lord has a plan for you

Depend on him for all things
No matter how big or small
With faith in Jesus Christ
You can have it all

One week following my diagnosis, Dr. Judy Tjoe met us with a warm smile. When I shook her hand, I knew she was the Breast Cancer Surgeon for me. As she explained the various treatment options, Dr. Tjoe demonstrated a high level of professionalism, concern, and compassion. I was impressed by her genuine sincerity. Before leaving that appointment, I offered to pray, she agreed, and we simultaneously reached for each other's hands.

As my mom and I proceeded out of the office, I thought to myself, *"Lord, I am not going to ask you, why me? But I am going to ask You to take me through this so I can be a blessing to someone else."*

And He did. He took me through. I considered my options and put them before the Lord in prayer. After praying one afternoon for guidance and confirmation regarding my choice of treatment, I received a phone call from my dear friend Rochelle. When I answered the phone, she said with boldness, *"Yo, the Lord told me to tell you, if it offends you, cut it off."*

She had no idea I was praying before her call. When she spoke those words, I felt relieved. I had my answer. I chose to have a bilateral mastectomy, which is the surgical removal of both breasts with reconstruction, which is surgery to rebuild the shape and look of the breast. Due to the early stage of breast cancer, I did not need chemotherapy or radiation. I thank God for taking me through this and using Rochelle to help me in my decision-making process.

Every challenge in life requires decisions. When those decisions are made without wisdom from the Word of God, it can lead to devastating results. My family and I chose to seek the knowledge of God through His Word, and those we trusted who had the mind of Christ. We didn't want to leave anything to chance; our lives depended on it. I believed God would carry me through the breast cancer diagnosis and help me choose the best treatment options for my body. I decided to have a bilateral mastectomy with reconstruction. My mother, diagnosed with stage two breast cancer, also sought the Lord. We both were led by God to follow a particular path. In the end, we both survived. To God, be the Glory!

The feelings of loneliness and depression can come upon you during trying times in life. But, it is during the times when you choose how you are going to cope. It is a choice. It is easy to decide to feel sorry for yourself or become angry. To cope effectively, I chose to read the Word of God, pray, and write poetry. Writing provided an outlet for me to freely express what and how I felt while walking by faith through breast cancer.

Reflection Questions
Do you seek counsel when you need it, or do you handle things alone? Think about it. Write it down.

_____

_____

_____

_____

_____

_____

_____

_____

_____

_____

_____

_____

_____

_____

_____

_____

_____

_____

_____

_____

_____

_____

_____

_____

Planted in the Word

Lord, I woke up early this morning
With my heart and mind on you
With tears rolling down my face
Giving thanks for what you have brought me through

Thank you for my family and friends
Thank you for showering me with their love
To receive from each of them
Has been a blessing from God above

At times it is overwhelming
To think about all they have done for me
Your Word says you will reap what you sow
I thank you for allowing me to sow years of loving seeds

Lord you knew what I would be going through
In October of 2007
My dad went from the hospital to a nursing home
To endure this, you gave me strength from heaven

While working a full-time job and going to school
In November of the same year
My mom was diagnosed with breast cancer
To endure this, you told me to cast down the spirit of fear

A few months later you lead me to ask
My doctor for a mammogram
I thought my mom was diagnosed, I was turning 40
It was time to schedule my first diagnostic breast exam.

I had the mammogram and other diagnostic tests
Of a small spot in my right breast
I said to myself, and everything will be fine
I'm just being put to a test

A week before my 40th birthday
I cried out to Jesus Christ
On the day I was diagnosed with Breast Cancer
A diagnosis that can change your life

Satan tried to destroy God's plan for me
He thought he could knock me down
He didn't know my mind was on Jesus
And my feet were planted in solid ground

You must be planted in the Word of God
To overcome obstacles that come your way
You must confess what the Word of God says
Confess His Word by faith every day

By His stripes, you are healed
When you are weak say I am strong
The Word of God will give you peace and strength
When everything appears to be going wrong

You are the head and not the tail
You are above and not beneath
Let the Word of God lead and guide you
Deliver and set you free

Spend time praying to the Lord
I am a witness. There is power in prayer
He will never leave you nor forsake you
God Almighty is always there

He is the healer of every sickness and disease
No matter what the doctors may say
Stay planted in the Word of God
Trust in Him and walk by faith

To stay planted in the Word of God was a choice. To have chosen to remain planted in God's word gave me peace, hope, and strength. I recall shortly after being diagnosed with breast cancer, one of my colleagues stopping at my desk, en route to her office, said,

"Yolanda, how are your mom and dad doing? I can't imagine anything else happening to you." At the time of this brief conversation, she and the rest of the nursing faculty were unaware of my breast cancer diagnosis. On this particular day, I was sitting at my desk, facing the computer, my back to my colleague. My sight became blurry due to the tears welling up in my eyes. All I could say over and over to myself, to keep tears from falling was, *"The joy of the Lord is my strength!" "The joy of the Lord is my strength!" "The joy of the Lord is my strength!"* At that moment, I could feel the tears drying up and the strength of the Lord, enabling me to reply to my co-worker with confidence. I believe words are powerful. In that moment of a potential emotional breakdown, I needed to keep it together by declaring and decreeing what I needed to experience to overcome the heaviness of that conversation.

Reflection Questions

What is your relationship like with the word of God, and what can you do to make it stronger? Think about it. Write it down.

_____

_____

_____

_____

_____

_____

_____

_____

_____

_____

_____

_____

_____

_____

_____

_____

_____

_____

_____

_____

_____

_____

_____

_____

_____

Declare and Decree It

Say what you want to see
You shall have whatsoever you say
Expect the promises of God
By activating your faith

There is power in the Word of God
Open your heart and receive
All things are possible
Unto him who believes

What are you believing God for
Speak it out of your mouth
Declare and decree it in the name of Jesus
Cast down all fear and doubt

Believe what is in your spirit
Do not deny what you see
Provision has already been made
God shall supply all your need

Is there anything too hard for God
The All-Sufficient and Mighty One
Trust God to bring it to pass
In Jesus name, it is already done

Is there anything too hard for God
There is nothing He can't do
You can do all things through Christ
It is He who strengthens you

Say what you want to see
You shall have whatsoever you say
Declare and decree it in Jesus name
Walkout God's plan for your life today

Words are powerful. They can make or break you. They can also build you up or tear you down. The Bible tells us in Proverbs 18:21 (KJV), *"Death and life are in the power of the tongue: and they that love it shall eat the fruit thereof."* Proverbs 18:21 in the Message version of the Bible reads: *Words kill, words give life; they're either poison or fruit—you choose.* I chose words that would give me life, words that would give me strength. Focusing on the Word of God during the challenging times of my life helped me to choose my words wisely.

Reflection Questions

Do you believe that your words can impact your life, if so how?
Think about it. Write it down.

_____

_____

_____

_____

_____

_____

_____

_____

_____

_____

_____

_____

_____

_____

_____

_____

_____

_____

_____

_____

_____

Never Alone

With God, you are never alone
He is always by your side
From the powerful presence of God
You are not able to hide

He sees what you are going through
He knows how you feel
No matter your situation or circumstances
Jesus Christ is real

You may not understand how things happen
Or why they have to be
I have learned to depend on God Almighty
And not my understanding

In the midst of it all God has a plan
Trust Him He is the light
His word is a lamp unto your feet
Walk by faith and not by sight

Allow His Spirit to comfort your heart
He will take you by the hand
He will provide everything to you need
Including the strength and courage to stand

Stand strong in the Lord and the power of His might
God through Christ Jesus provides the way
To overcome and conquer the challenges
You may face from day to day

One powerful reality for Christians is the fact that God is eternally present with us.

"...for He [God] Himself has said, I will not in any way fail you nor give you up nor leave you without support. [I will] not, [I will] not, [I will] not in any degree leave you helpless nor forsake nor let [you] down (relax My hold on you)! [Assuredly not!] Hebrews 13:6b AMPC

God's presence was with me during those trying years as I walked through the traumas of my life and that of my parents. There is no possible way that I could have imagined going through all I have without God being ever-present. His word and peace were my constant companions, and they kept my mind and heart. His joy became my strength (Nehemiah, 8:10).

Another individual with me throughout the entire ordeal was Deon, my high school sweetheart. At the time, we were just dating, but from the moment I shared my battle with cancer, his love and concern never waned. He walked with me every step of the way, and two years after the breast cancer diagnosis, we married, and I became Mrs. Deon Sartin.

In 2011, Dr. Tjoe asked me to participate in a 12-week training program that would prepare breast cancer survivors to complete a sprint distance triathlon, which included a half-mile open water swim, 15-mile bike ride, and 3.1-mile run. I agreed to do it. That group of survivors became what is now known to Aurora Health Care, as Team Phoenix. I thank God for the opportunity to train for and complete a triathlon.

Reflective Questions

What do you do when you feel alone? Think about it. Write it down.

_____

_____

_____

_____

_____

_____

_____

_____

_____

List 3 people you know would support you in troubled times? Think about it. Write it down.

_____

_____

_____

_____

_____

_____

_____

_____

_____

A Purpose for Your Life

As a child of the Most-High God
You have been blessed by our Father above
With wisdom, strength, and confidence
Assurance, peace, and love

There is a purpose for your life
There is a reason why you are here
Do not let your age be a distraction
Nor the spirit of fear

God gave you the spirit of love
Power and of a sound mind
You are to be used for the glory of God
When? Now is the time

There is a purpose for your life
There are greater works for you to do
Trust and depend on the spirit of God
To ultimately lead and guide you

Let God Almighty use you
Beyond your imagination
Expect to reach those around you
And those in other nations

Share what God has done in your life
Someone needs to know
Tell them God is able
Your testimony will help them to grow

Expect to fulfill what God has called you to do
There is a purpose for your life
Expect to live out God's plan for you
In the name of Jesus Christ

I vividly remember a day in 1994, while sitting in my office, working as a Counselor Supervisor for a residential treatment facility for children with behavioral problems. I was overwhelmed with the realization that my job was no longer fulfilling. I felt an inner life shift, and I knew I had more to give. I graduated from Drake University with a degree in psychology and was honorably discharged as a second lieutenant from the United States Army, but I felt there was more. I enjoyed working as a Counselor Supervisor for nearly four years, but my heart was no longer content. There was a deeper yearning inside of me to make a significant impact in the lives of others. I didn't know what to do, so I prayed, asking, *"Lord, what is your purpose for my life? What do you want me to do now? Please tell me."*

When I asked God to reveal His purpose, I expected Him to respond. I needed His Spirit to lead and guide me as I pursued the unknown contents of my heart. I didn't have a clue of what was stirring in me. I did, however, know my season of working as a Counselor Supervisor was quickly coming to an end. During that transitional season, I decided to spend quality time with God, in His Word, and prayer.

Not knowing what was next, I unconsciously obeyed 1 Thessalonians 5:18, *"In everything give thanks: for this is the will of God in Christ Jesus concerning you."* I thanked God daily for plainly revealing my next steps. As a result, the desire to do more for others grew deeper and stronger.

One day, I grabbed the newspaper and began looking in the classified section for job opportunities (google didn't exist). Paging through, I was amazed to see the abundance of job postings for nurses. There were available nursing jobs in hospitals, nursing homes, clinics, and home health care agencies. I was intrigued. There was a quickening in my spirit.

Looking at the nursing opportunities allowed my heart to open to the possibility and reality of a significant career change. I could see myself in the role of a nurse, enjoying and caring for others. Every day for nearly two weeks after reading the classified section, I encountered a Registered Nurse (RN). I knew those brief interactions were God-ordained. It didn't matter where I went; I crossed paths with a nurse in a gas station, grocery store, beauty supply store, and at church. I even ran into an old friend with her mother, who also happened to be a registered nurse, but I didn't know until that time. With each interaction, there was a sense of joy and excitement that blazed inside of me. My prayers took on new meaning; they were more direct and focused. I knew in my heart, the Spirit of God was leading and guiding me to go back to school. This time, it would be in the field of nursing. I realized the yearning I had to care for others was God's desire to use me as a registered nurse. Within a few days of that experience, I applied to a local nursing school program and began my journey to become a registered nurse.

Reflection Questions

What is your purpose? Think about it. Write it down.

_____

_____

_____

_____

_____

_____

_____

_____

_____

_____

Who are you called to impact? Think about it. Write it down.

_____

_____

_____

_____

_____

_____

_____

_____

_____

_____

_____

_____

Desires of Your Heart

You have been called out of darkness
And into the marvelous light
Let the Word of God shine through you
Like a beacon in the night

Set yourself aside
Let God have His way
Allow His will for your life
To be carried out from day to day

Seek God's guidance in prayer
Meditate on His Word
Listen for that soft still voice
Listen until it is heard

Trust in God and have faith in Him
He has given you what you have
The vision He placed deep in your heart
In due time will come to pass

Have faith in what God has given you to do
Live out your hopes and dreams
Faith is the substance of things hoped for
And the evidence of things not seen

Let God have total control
He has been with you from the start
Delight yourself also in the Lord
And He will give you the desires of your heart

"Delight yourself also in the Lord, And He shall give you the desires of your heart. Commit your way to the Lord, Trust also in Him, And He shall bring it to pass." Psalm 37:4-5 (NKJV)

To delight yourself in the Lord means to find peace and fulfillment in your heart in Christ. To trust also in Him means that you have a firm belief in His strength and His reliability. When you trust the Lord with your heart's desires, He will bring them to pass. No matter how long it takes, or the obstacles you may endure along the way, we have His promise, He will bring them to pass.

My heart's desire was to become a registered nurse. While I was in nursing school, I worked at a hospital in Milwaukee, Wisconsin, as a Certified Nursing Assistant (CNA), and I loved it. I enjoyed the simplest of things; talking to patients, helping them get in and out of bed, and assisting them with walking. I enjoyed it all, but my heart longed to become a registered nurse.

When I graduated from nursing school, I continued to work with patients in the role of a graduate nurse until I passed the state licensure exam. A Graduate nurse is assigned to work with a registered nurse to learn further hands-on responsibilities of being a nurse. A graduate nurse becomes registered after he/she successfully passes the state nursing board exam. This exam is a standardized test that every state regulatory board uses to determine if a candidate is ready to become licensed as an entry-level nurse. It is a computerized test that requires the candidate to answer a minimum of 75 questions to a maximum of 265.

Reflective Questions

What desires do you have that no one knows about? Think about it. Write it down.

_____

_____

_____

_____

_____

_____

_____

_____

What would you do if there were no obstacles in your way? Think about it. Write it down.

_____

_____

_____

_____

_____

_____

_____

_____

_____

_____

_____

When Challenges Arise

When faced with challenges as we often are
Look to be led by the Bright Shining Star

God will comfort you and take you by the hand
and provide courage, peace, and strength to stand

His spirit will speak directly to your heart
informing you on how and where to start

God will give you wisdom and understanding when you ask in faith
And the desire and patience to wait without haste

When challenges arise He will ease your mind
You will not go into a situation completely blind

God will open your eyes and allow you to see
What must be done to gain the victory

He will guide your thoughts and make away
With God, you will not be lead astray

Challenges may overwhelm you
Just breathe with God, there is nothing you can't do

Be strong and of good courage, do not fear nor be afraid of them; for
the Lord your God, He is the One who goes with you. He will not
leave you nor forsake you." Deuteronomy 31:6 NLT

I found comfort in knowing God through His Spirit was with me. He accompanied me to every doctor's appointment. He was there during every surgical procedure. God was with me throughout all recovery periods and multiple surgeries resulting from breast cancer. I never felt alone because He never left me alone.

When I went to take my state board exam, it seemed as though the test would never end. The questions kept popping on the screen, one after another. Finally, after about four hours, the agony of testing was over. I had to wait several weeks for the results to arrive in the mail. After some time, several of my peers received their passing results in the mail. Shortly after that, my results came. I opened the big brown envelope, and my heart sank as I read the results. I did not pass. I was very disappointed, but I didn't cry. I received a call from a classmate a few days prior, and she shared that she had not passed the exam. I thought to myself; I will retake it. At that time, I had to wait three months to retest. While waiting, I continued to work as a graduate nurse. However, with the retesting date quickly approaching, I could feel the weight of test anxiety rising in my neck and shoulders. During that time, I kept myself busy to keep my mind from thinking about the failing results, and I continued to review nursing content and practice exam questions.

Before taking the exam the second time, I began to reflect on the test anxiety I experienced while attending Drake University. During my second semester at Drake, I was taking a calculus class. This class, for me, was very challenging. I found the content complicated to understand. I had a tutor for the course. However, I recall walking in the classroom on the morning of my first calculus exam. I sat in a seat next to a window. The professor took his time distributing test booklets to each student, one by one. When I received the booklet, I felt the spirit of anxiety and fear overtake me. I could feel the muscles in my neck, tightening up. When I opened the booklet, the questions looked as though written in a foreign language. My hands were sweaty, and I felt like throwing up. I put my head down, took a deep breath, and did the best I could do. After the exam, I felt awful. My head was pounding. I left the class with tears in my eyes and went to speak with a counselor to discuss changing my major from Pre-med to Psychology.

The flashback of that unforgettable experience kept entering and leaving my mind before taking the licensure exam for the second time. After weeks of waiting for a second time, the envelope arrived. I ripped it open, only to once again find failing results. My heart sank deeper, and the tears began to roll down my face. I felt defeated and began to question my ability to become a registered nurse. I felt like giving up. But in my heart, the Lord reminded me of His plan for me to be a nurse, which meant that giving up was not an option. The process of me becoming a nurse was a process that I had to persevere through.

Reflection Questions

Have you ever felt like a failure? Think about it. Write it down.

_____

_____

_____

_____

_____

_____

_____

_____

_____

_____

Name three things you can tell yourself when you feel like a failure. Think about it. Write it Down.

_____

_____

_____

_____

_____

_____

_____

_____

_____

_____

_____

Don't Give Up

When times are difficult
And you don't know what to do
Maintain your strength
Believe in you

Do not get discouraged
Don't entertain negative thoughts
Develop a Positive Attitude
This is what it's all about

Don't let the situation
Take control of your mind
You must hold on and take it
One day at a time

You can't let what others say
Knock you to the ground
People will do anything
To try to keep you down

Don't Give Up
When things are hard to do
Put your faith in Christ
Let Him carry you through

Walk by Faith
Not by Sight
All things are possible
Through our Lord Jesus Christ

It is easy to give up and quit when a situation becomes frustrating, or a mountain seems too hard to climb. It can also be easy to abandon a cause when you experience failure trying to succeed. When you work hard to accomplish something, giving it your all and best, you will have days when thoughts of quitting bombard your mind.

During those times, step back, take a moment. Allow yourself to feel the heaviness and disappointment of failing. But don't stay there, choose not to carry the weight of disappointment or view yourself through the lens of failure. Choose to believe, despite the disappointment, because you are more than a conqueror. Choose to accept what was, while at the same time settling that no matter how many times you may fail in the process of working towards your dream, you are not a failure. Don't give up!

"Jesus said to him, "if you can believe, all things are possible to him who believes." Mark 9:23 NKJV

Reflective Questions

When have you ever felt like giving up? Share the experience.
Think about it. Write it down.

_____

_____

_____

_____

_____

_____

_____

_____

What would you say to someone who wanted to give up? How
would you encourage them? Think about it. Write down?

_____

_____

_____

_____

_____

_____

_____

_____

_____

Believe and Receive

Speak those things as though they were
By faith, they shall be
What things so ever you desire when you pray
Believe and receive

Speak those things as though they were
Speak it out of your mouth my faith
Be it unto you according to His word
You shall have whatsoever you say

Call it out in the name of Jesus
Call it in unto you
Look past what you see Look to God
There is nothing He can't do

Life and death are in the power of the tongue
In your situation speak life
You are anointed by God and blessed to be a blessing
In the name of Jesus Christ

Position yourself to obey His word
Do not doubt in your heart receive
Take steps toward your heart's desire
All things are possible unto him who believes

Walk by faith and not by sight
Do what God has called you to do.
Have faith, pray, believe and receive
All God has for you.

Your perception of a situation that appears to be too overwhelming to endure can be a distraction from the enemy. Jesus reminds us in John 10:10, *"The thief does not come except to steal, and to kill and to destroy."*

As it relates to your dreams, the enemy desires to steal your faith, kill your joy, and destroy your life as you pursue your dreams. But thank God, Jesus came making abundant life available to us all. I love the amplified version of John 10:10 because it reads: *"The thief comes only in order to steal and kill and destroy. I came that they may have and enjoy life, and have it in abundance [to the full, till it overflows]."*

That is the kind of life God wants for you and me. After reading this scripture repeatedly, faith rose within me, giving me a bold determination. I could not quit. So I decided to take the exam for the third time.

I studied and studied for the exam in preparation for my third go-round. The same process, weeks go by, anticipation rises, and finally, the envelope arrives in the mail. (This was years before my Father's illness or my mother's diagnosis.) Holding the envelope in hand, I looked at my parents and took the envelope up to my room. Closing the door, I sat on my bed and slowly opened the envelope. When I pulled out the failing results, I emotionally lost it.

I recall lying on my bed in the fetal position, crying hard and uncontrollably. My dad rushed up the stairs and burst into my room. He stood in the doorway speechless, trying to find the right words to say to me. But the more he tried, the louder I cried. He eventually turned and left my room, sending my mother. I was devastated. I couldn't believe it. I knew God put the desire to become a registered nurse in my heart; I knew it. But the dream in my heart didn't match the current reality of my life, and I couldn't make sense of it. And after three attempts leading to failures, I began to question whether or not I had heard from God after all.

Reflection Questions

What thoughts have you had to cast down in order to push past perceived failure in order to believe you receive? Think about it. Write it down.

_____

_____

_____

_____

_____

_____

_____

_____

_____

What are you currently believing you will achieve or receive? Think about it. Write it down.

_____

_____

_____

_____

_____

_____

_____

_____

_____

You, Will Make It

You will make it Have no fear
When you are down and out, the Lord is near

When you want to give up and completely let go
Look in the mirror and tell yourself "NO"

Through difficult times you will succeed
Our Father above will provide your need

Depend on Him in all you do
Trust and believe He will carry you through

You will make it do not doubt
For you, God Almighty will make a way out

When God has a plan for your life, quitting is not an option. My pastor once said, "*As Christians, we didn't give ourselves God's plan, and when we walk with Him through troubled times, neither should we permit ourselves to abort the plan.*"

When the road gets rough, and you cannot see your way, you can choose to throw in the towel, or you can choose to trust God and walk by faith. I decided on the latter. I decided to allow the Spirit of God to lead and guide me. His spirit led me through that challenging time, along with powerful, uplifting words of encouragement from my family and close friends.

Before taking the national licensure exam for the fourth time, one of my close friends reminded me of who I was in Christ and what I could do through Him. My friend said, "*Yolanda, you are more than a conqueror (Romans 8:37); With God, nothing is impossible (Luke*

1:37); Yolanda, you can do all things through Christ who strengthens you (Philippians 4:13)." That was enough for me. I had the word of God to remind me of who I was, and I had the support of family and friends. The victory was mine!

Reflection Questions

What are three things you would say to encourage yourself to hang in there and not quit? Think about it. Write it down.

1._____

_____

_____

_____

_____

_____

2._____

_____

_____

_____

_____

_____

3._____

_____

_____

_____

_____

_____

There is Power in Your Words

When you abide in Him
And God's word abides in you
The Spirit of the living God
Will lead and guide you into all truth

When you trust in the word of God
And open your heart to receive
You will find all things are possible
Unto him who believes

There is power in the word of God
There is power when you speak it by faith
According to the word of God
You shall have whatsoever you say

Let the weak say I am strong
Let the bound say I am free
Let the poor say I am rich
It is God who supplies all your need

Let the sick say I am healed
You are healed by the blood of the lamb
God is the healer of every sickness and disease
Nothing is too hard for the great I AM

Trust in the word of God
God said cast upon Him your cares
God is waiting to hear from you
Take time to commune with Him in prayer

I should have listened. After my second and third unsuccessful attempts at passing the exam, a friend advised me to take an exam review course, but regrettably, I didn't. I should have listened, and today, I still wonder why? Somehow unconsciously, although anxious, each time I thought I was ready. So this time, I heeded my friend's advice and registered for a review course in preparation for the state nursing board exam. I was taking it for the fourth time.

I had everything to lose. A week or so before taking the exam, my supervisor called me into her office. She informed me pleasantly and professionally that if I did not pass the exam on this attempt, she would have to demote me to my former status as CNA. With tears in my eyes, I told her I was determined to pass the exam. However, if I did not, I informed her that she would not need to demote me because I would resign altogether. I excused myself at the end of our conversation and went back to work.

At that moment, I seemed defeated but chose not to feel defeated. I could not imagine working once again as a CNA after pursuing a bachelor's of science degree in nursing and seeing myself inwardly as an RN. The two realities for me did not match. As I walked, I said to myself, "*Yolanda, you are going to be an excellent nurse. You are going to make a difference in the lives of many people. You cannot and will not quit.*" Through the power of my words, I became more determined to pass the nursing board exam successfully than in previous times before.

Reflection Question

What words of confession can you write to declare and decree over your own life? Think about it. Write it down.

_____

_____

_____

_____

_____

_____

_____

_____

_____

_____

_____

_____

_____

_____

_____

_____

_____

_____

_____

The Power of Visualization

There is power in visualization
Focus on what you want to be
If you believe in your visual concept
You can make it a reality

If a runner visualizes losing
Before and during a race
The negative attitude and lack of focus
Will throw the runner off the pace

If the runner thinks he can win
And knows he has what it takes
His positive attitude, determination, and focus
Will enable him to win the race

Take the time to visualize
What you see can come true
The sky's the limit
Choose to believe in you

Take action on your visual concept
Choose to impact nations
Imagine yourself where you want to be
There is power in visualization

During the last couple of weeks before taking the exam for the fourth time, I declined invitations to gather with family and friends. I turned down opportunities to watch television. Instead, I used my time reviewing hundreds of nursing practice questions. I poured myself into studying the nursing content, going over what I learned from the review course. I surrounded myself with positive people and confessed Philippians 4:13; I *can do all things through Christ, who strengthens me and* Luke 1:37. With *God, nothing is impossible."*

I took time daily to meditate on the Word of God, thinking positively about the exam. I visualized myself calmly walking into the testing area, politely taking my seat and praying before starting. I then imagined myself successfully passing the exam. I was more determined than ever.

Reflection Questions

Visualize yourself doing what you desire to do, what do you see? Think about it. Write it/them down.

_____

_____

_____

_____

_____

_____

_____

_____

_____

What three steps will you take in the next three months toward doing what you visualize yourself doing? Think about it. Write it/them down.

_____

_____

_____

_____

_____

_____

_____

_____

_____

Conquer Your Challenges

You have the potential
To achieve and excel
Get all you can out of life
In all you do, do it well

Think highly of yourself
Take pride in all you do
The dream you have to succeed
Make your dream come true

Do not get discouraged
When challenges come your way
Bow your head and plow forward
Conquer your challenges each day

Have faith in your abilities
In yourself, you must believe
If you believe in you
There is nothing you can't achieve

Take time, look in the mirror
Realize you are who you are
Look at your positive attributes
Allow them to stand out like a bright shining star

Stand firm in the name of success
Plant your feet on solid ground
You are encouraged to conquer your challenges
As you strive forward, bound

The exam day finally arrived. All I could say that day was, *"Lord, have your way."* I did not allow the spirit of fear or anxiety to overtake me. Before starting the exam, I took a few deep breaths, reminded myself of who I was in Christ Jesus, and said a brief prayer. I then proceeded to answer the questions one after another with undeniable confidence. Before I realized it, I had responded to over one hundred and fifty questions, but then suddenly, the computer just shut off. I didn't know what to think. I figured maybe I had answered enough questions for them to determine if I passed or failed. So I chose to believe I passed the exam.

God called me to be a nurse, to care for others competently, with patience, love, and compassion. Had I known how challenging it was going to be to become a registered nurse, I don't believe I would have taken this path. However, God knows what he's doing in our lives, and He does not give us more than we can handle. You must understand that even if you fail at something multiple times, it does not make you a failure because God made you more than a conqueror.

Yet in all things, we are more than conquerors through Him who loves us Romans 8:37 (NKJV).

God's power within us is amazing! Through Christ Jesus, we are more than able to conquer challenges. We have the victory. Half the battle is believing that you are more than a conqueror and doing so smack dab in the middle of what appears to be failure or defeat.

Reflection Questions

In what way can you educate yourself to better prepare you for your future? Think about it. Write it down.

_____

_____

_____

_____

_____

_____

_____

_____

_____

How will you handle an unexpected failure moving forward? Think about it. Write it down.

_____

_____

_____

_____

_____

_____

_____

_____

_____

The Victory is Won

Look at yourself and smile
Look at what you have done
This battle you fought is over
Praise God the victory is won

Many thought you would not make it
Many thought you would not succeed
God says you are more than a conqueror
You are intelligent and smart indeed

With God nothing is impossible
With God, you cannot go wrong
When you feel like giving up
The Spirit of God will make you strong

You have what it takes to succeed
There is nothing you can't do
As you continue to strive to reach your highest goals
Let the Spirit of God lead and guide you

Focus your heart and mind
To live out your heart's desire
Your steps are ordered by the Lord
He will take you higher

They say the third time's a charm, but for me, it was the fourth. After several weeks of waiting, one day, while at work, I looked down the main hallway on a unit I had been assigned. Surprisingly both my father and my younger brother were walking toward me. My heart sank as I saw the large manila envelope in my father's hand. It was my results. I instructed my parents, whom I still lived with at the time, not to open the envelope when it arrived, so my father brought it to me. I began walking quickly towards them. As I approached my dad and my brother, I grabbed them both by the arms and pulled them into an empty room and asked: *"Why are you here"?* With tears welling up in my dad's eyes, he gave me the envelope. My hands began to shake as I slowly opened it. When I saw the results, I S-C-R-E-A-M-E-D, and I mean, I screamed loud running down the hall. When my co-workers heard the scream, they thought something was drastically wrong with one of the patients and quickly came running. I screamed again and shouted, *"I PASSED!" "I PASSED!" "I PASSED THE NURSING BOARD EXAM!"*

Several of the nurses who knew my situation shared in the joy of that moment. That was a day I will never forget, and I will forever thank God for the victory.

Reflection Questions

Are you willing to persevere and pursue no matter how long it takes? Think about it. Write it down.

_____

_____

_____

_____

_____

_____

_____

_____

_____

_____

_____

_____

_____

_____

_____

_____

_____

_____

_____

_____

_____

To Be Persistent

To be persistent in the name of Jesus
At times can be hard to do
Stand fast and focus on God
Expect Him to carry you through

Ask, and it shall be given
Seek, and ye shall find
Knock, and the door shall be opened unto you
Regardless of the day or the time

It is God's will for you to be persistent
It is God's will for you to stand
Walk by faith and not by sight
By holding on to the Savior's hand

Your steps are ordered by the Lord
Your way has already been made
Be persistent in the things of God
By seeking His guidance each day

Be steadfast and unmovable
Always abounding in the work of the Lord
Be persistent in the things of God
Walk with Him on one accord

Many walked with me through that time and space, but no one was as encouraging as my mom. I am so grateful for her persistent encouragement during that time in my life. When I entertained the thought of not retaking the exam, my mom was right there, telling me not to give up. I can hear her words today, *"Yolanda, keep retesting until you pass the exam."* To this day, I thank God for her persistence and loving support.

It takes perseverance to persevere and pursue your heart's desire, especially when significant challenges arise. To go to work, day after day, resisting feelings and thoughts of shame and defeat were not easy for me. It was the strength of God that enabled me to persevere and the peace of God that allowed me to pursue taking the exam until I passed.

Reflection Questions

What are you persistent about doing today? Think about it. Write it down.

_____

_____

_____

_____

_____

_____

_____

_____

What behaviors do you currently have that sabotage your consistency? Think about it. Write it down.

_____

_____

_____

_____

_____

_____

_____

_____

_____

_____

Pursue It!

Do not be afraid to do says the Lord
What I have put in you to do
Your obedience to God's voice is connected
To someone else's breakthrough

Your way may not be clear
You may not know which route to take
Trust me says the spirit of God
This will be a walk of faith

Be encouraged to spend time in the word of God
Be inspired to seek my face
As you pursue what I put in you to do says the Lord
The spirit of God will guide your way

Be quick to hear what I say says the Lord
What you hear and do will affect many lives
You will reach the nations says the Lord
Your ministry in Jesus name is worldwide

In me is everything you need says the Lord
Ask and believe you receive
Fast and pray as you obey what God says
Worship Him and give God the glory

Whatever is in your heart to do, pursue it. No matter how long it takes, don't give up. Be encouraged to walk out your visions and dreams with God as your guide. Remember, He gave those visions and dreams to you. God will be with you every step of the way. Persevere and pursue, do what is in your heart to do!